That Make a

무당벌레

Ashley Lee

Explore other books at:
WWW.ENGAGEBOOKS.COM

VANCOUVER, B.C.

e WWW.ENGAGEBOOKS.COM

Ladybugs: Level 1 Bilingual (English/Korean) (영어/한국어)
Animals That Make a Difference!
Lee, Ashley 1995 –
Text © 2021 Engage Books
Edited by: A.R. Roumanis
and Lauren Dick
Translated by: Gio Oh
Proofread by: Tamara Kazali

Text set in Arial Regular.
Chapter headings set in Arial Black.

FIRST EDITION / FIRST PRINTING

LIBRARY AND ARCHIVES CANADA CATALOGUING IN PUBLICATION

Title: Animals That Make a Difference: Ladybugs Level 1 Bilingual (English/Korean) (영어/한국어)
Names: Lee, Ashley, author.

ISBN 978-1-77476-459-6 (hardcover)
ISBN 978-1-77476-458-9 (softcover)

Subjects:
LCSH: Ladybugs—Juvenile literature
LCSH: Human-animal relationships—Juvenile literature

Classification: LCC QL596.C65 L44 2020 | DDC J595.76/9—DC23

Contents
목차

What Are Ladybugs?
무당벌레는 무엇인가요?

Ladybugs are a kind of beetle. They are also called lady beetles or ladybirds.
무당벌레는 딱정벌레의 일종입니다. 레이디비틀즈나 레이디버드라고도 불립니다.

Ladybugs are very helpful to people, other animals, and Earth.

무당벌레는 사람들, 다른 동물들 그리고 지구에게도 매우 도움이 됩니다.

What Do Ladybugs Look Like?
무당벌레는 어떻게 생겼나요?

Ladybugs are only 0.4 inches (1 centimeter) long. Most ladybugs are red, orange, or yellow. Some ladybugs have black or red spots.

무당벌레는0.4인치(1센티미터)밖에 되지 않습니다. 대부분의 무당벌레들은 빨강, 주황 노란색이에요. 어떤 무당벌레들은 검은색이나 빨간반점이 있기도 해요.

Ladybugs have feelers on their heads. They are used to smell, taste, and touch.

무당벌레는 머리에 더듬이가 있어요. 냄새를 맡고 맛을 보고 만지는데에 사용해요.

A ladybug's front wings are hard and brightly colored. They protect the back wings.

무당벌레의 앞날개는 단단하고 밝은 색이에요. 뒷날개를 보호하기도 합니다.

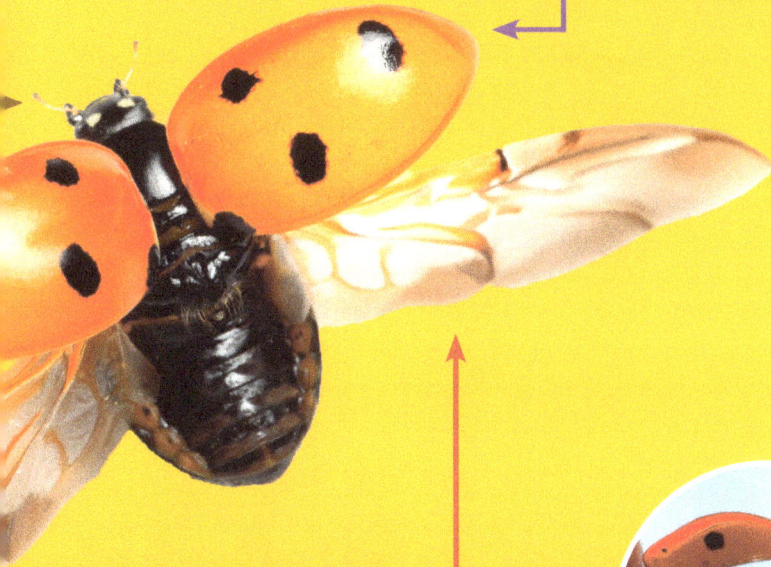

A ladybug's back wings are four times larger than their bodies. They stay folded under the front wings until it is time to fly.

무당벌레의 뒷날개는 몸보다 4배 큽니다. 날기 전까지 앞 날개 아래에 접혀 있어요.

Where Do Ladybugs Live?
무당벌레는 어디서 사나요?

Ladybugs live all over the word.
They make their homes in trees,
bushes, or gardens.
무당벌레는 전 세계 어디든 살고있어요.
나무, 덤불 또는 정원에서 살아요.

Pink spotted ladybugs are found in the United States. Mexican bean beetles come from Mexico. Three-banded ladybugs are found in Europe.

분홍색 점을 가진 무당벌레가 미국에서 발견 됐어요. 멕시코 콩 딱정벌레는 멕시코에서 왔어요. 삼띠무당벌레는 유럽에서 발견 됐어요.

Atlantic Ocean
북극해

Europe
유럽

United States
미국

Europe
유럽

North America
북아메리카

Atlantic Ocean
대서양

Asia
아시아

Africa
아프리카

Indian Ocean
인도양

South America
남아메리카

Mexico
멕시코

Pacific Ocean
태평양

Southern Ocean
남대양

2,000 miles
2,000 마일
0

4,000 kilometers
4,000 킬로미터
0

N

Legend 전설
■ Land 육지
□ Ocean 바다

9

What Do Ladybugs Eat?
무당벌레는 무엇을 먹나요?

Ladybugs eat smaller insects. Most ladybugs eat tiny insects called aphids.

무당벌레는 작은 곤충을 잡아먹어요.
대부분 무당벌레는 진딧물이라고
불리는 작은 곤충을 먹어요.

Some ladybugs eat mushrooms or leaves.
어떤 무당벌레들은 버섯이나 잎을 먹기도 합니다.

Ladybugs do not chew up and down. They chew side to side.
무당벌레는 위아래로 씹지않고 나란히 씹습니다.

11

How Do Ladybugs Talk to Each Other?
무당벌레는 서로 어떻게 이야기하나요?

Ladybugs make smelly chemicals called pheromones. They put these chemicals around their homes. The smell can attract other ladybugs or warn them of danger.

무당벌레는 페로몬이라고 불리는 냄새나는 화학물질을 만들어요. 이 화학물질을 집 주변에 뿌립니다. 이 냄새는 다른 무당벌레를 유인하거나 위험을 경고할 수 있어요.

Ladybugs can release liquid from their legs. The liquid tastes very bad and warns larger animals not to eat them.

무당벌레는 다리에서 액체를 만들 수 있어요. 이 액체는 맛이 매우 안 좋기 때문에 다른 동물들이 무당벌레를 잡아먹지 않습니다.

Ladybug Life Cycle
무당벌레의 일생

Ladybugs can lay hundreds of eggs at one time. Ladybug eggs hatch after 2 to 5 days.
무당벌레는 한번에 수백 개의 알을 낳을 수 있어요. 무당벌레의 알은 2일이나 5일후에 부화합니다.

Baby ladybugs are called larvae. They look like tiny alligators.
아기 무당벌레는 유충이라고 불러요. 유충은 작은 악어처럼 보이기도해요.

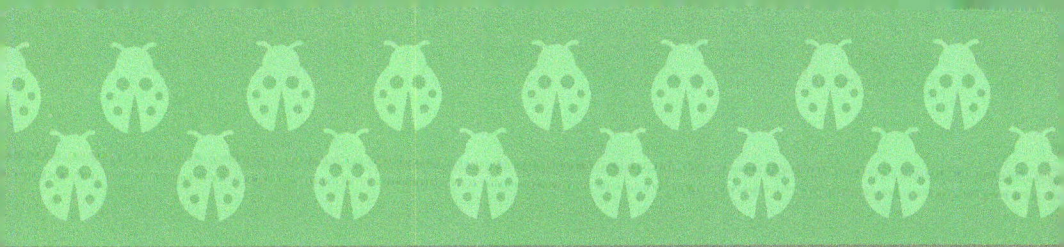

Larvae create hard shells around their bodies.
Larvae in shells are called pupae. Pupae stay
in their shells for about a week.
껍데기안에 있는 유충은 번데기라고 불러요. 껍데기안에
있는 유충은 번데기라고 불러요. 번데기는 약 일주일 동안
껍데기 안에 있습니다.

Ladybugs are adults
when they crawl out of
their hard shells. They
live for 2 to 3 years.
껍질에서 나온 무당벌레는
성체입니다. 2년에서
3년동안 살아요.

Curious Facts About Ladybugs

Ladybugs cannot fly in temperatures below 55° fahrenheit (13° celsius).
무당벌레는 화씨55도 (섭씨13도) 이하의 온도에서는 날수 없어요.

Ladybugs hibernate during winter. This means they sleep until the weather gets warmer.
무당벌레는 겨울 동안 겨울잠을 자요. 이 뜻은 날씨가 따뜻해질 때까지 잠을 잔다는 말입니다.

The spots on a ladybug fade as they get older.
나이가 들수록 등에 있는 반점은 희미해집니다.

무당벌레에 대한 흥미로운 사실들

One ladybug will eat almost 5,000 insects during its life.
한 무당벌레는 일생동안 거의 5,000마리의 곤충을 먹습니다.

NASA sent ladybugs to space in 1999.
나사는 1999년에 무당벌레를 우주로 보냈어요.

Ladybugs beat their wings about 85 times every second when they fly.
무당벌레는 날 때마다 매초 85번 정도 날개짓을 합니다.

Kinds of Ladybugs
무당벌레의 종류

There are around 5,000 kinds of ladybugs. Some kinds of ladybugs have lots of spots. Some have no spots at all.

무당벌레의 종류는 약 5,000가지가 있습니다. 어떤 종류의 무당벌레들은 많은 무늬들을 가지고 있습니다. 어떤 무당벌레는 아예 없습니다.

2-spot ladybugs are one of the most common ladybugs. They can be red with black spots or black with red spots.

이성 무당벌레는 가장 흔한 종류입니다. 빨간 바탕에 검은 점 또는 검은 바탕에 빨간 점이 있기도 합니다.

22-spotted ladybugs are yellow with black spots. They are one of the few ladybugs that eat mushrooms.
22성무당벌레는 노란 바탕에 검은 점입니다. 이 무당벌레는 버섯을 먹는 몇 안되는 무당벌레 중 하나입니다.

Steelblue ladybugs only live in Australia and New Zealand. They do not have any spots.
강철 무당벌레는 호주와 뉴질랜드에서만 삽니다.
강철 무당벌레는 아무런 무늬가 없어요.

How Ladybugs Help Earth
무당벌레가 지구를 돕는 방법

Aphids are tiny bugs that eat and poison plants. Ladybugs help get rid of aphids so plants can grow.
진딧물은 식물을 먹기도하고 감염도 시키는 작은 벌레에요. 무당벌레는 식물이 잘 자랄 수 있도록 진딧물을 없애줘요.

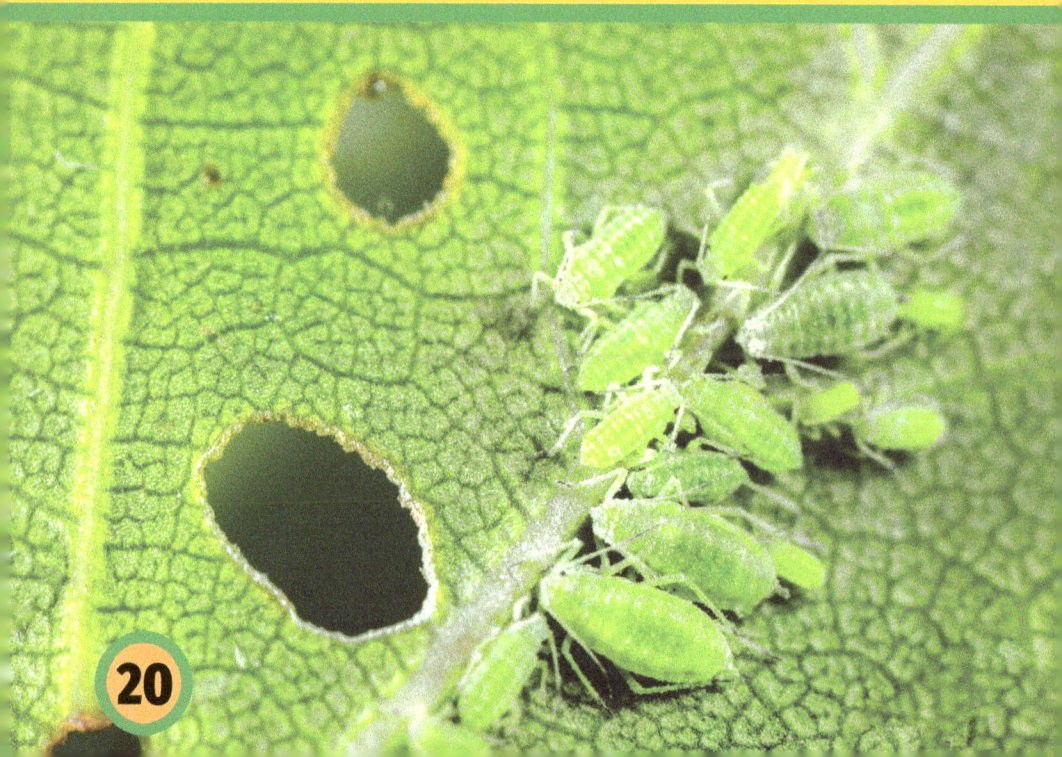

Ladybugs lay their eggs in areas with lots of aphids. Ladybug larvae eat the aphids when they hatch.

무당벌레는 진딧물이 많은 곳에 알을 낳아요. 무당벌레의 유충이 부화하면 진딧물을 잡아먹어요.

How Ladybugs Help
Other Animals
무당벌레가 다른 동물을 돕는 방법

Some farmers use chemicals to get rid of bugs that harm plants. These chemicals can make animals sick.
몇몇 농부들은 농작물을 해치는 벌레들을 없애기 위해 화학물질을 사용해요. 이 화학물질이 동물들을 병들게 할 수 있어요.

Ladybugs eat these harmful bugs. This means farmers do not have to use as many chemicals.

무당벌레가 이 해충들을 잡아 먹어요. 이는 농부들이 더이상 화학 물질을 사용할 필요가 없단 뜻입니다.

How Ladybugs Help Humans
무당벌레가 사람을 돕는 방법

Aphids can destroy entire fields of food if left alone.
진딧물은 혼자 있어도 전체 농작물을 파괴 할 수 있습니다.

People would have a hard time growing food without ladybugs.

사람들은 무당벌레의 도움이 없다면 작물을 기르는 것이 힘들거에요.

Ladybugs in Danger
멸종위기의 무당벌레

The Asian ladybug was brought to North America from Asia by humans. They chase other ladybugs away from their homes.

아시아 무당벌레는 인간들이 아시아에서 미국으로 데려왔어요. 나머지 무당벌레들은 고향에서 따라왔죠.

The nine-spotted ladybug has started disappearing. The Asian ladybug is eating all their food and taking over their homes.

구성무당벌레는 사라지기 시작했어요. 아시아 무당벌레가 집을 차지하고 음식도 다 먹어치우고 있기 때문이죠.

How To Help Ladybugs
무당벌레를 돕는 방법

People are helping ladybugs by planting colorful flowers. This attracts ladybugs and gives them a safe place to live. Most ladybugs like marigolds, cosmos, and calendula.

사람들은 여러 색의 꽃을 키움으로서 무당벌레를 돕고 있어요. 이는 무당벌레를 유혹해서 살 곳을 마련해줘요. 대부분의 무당벌레는 마리골드 코스모스 카렌듈라를 좋아해요.

Many people build ladybug houses. This gives ladybugs a safe place to sleep.
많은 사람들이 무당벌레의 집을 지어요.
무당벌레가 잠을 잘 수 있는 안전한 곳이 되죠.

Quiz
퀴즈

Test your knowledge of ladybugs by answering the following questions. The questions are based on what you have read in this book. The answers are listed on the bottom of the next page.

다음 질문에 답하고 무당벌레에 대한 지식을 테스트해봐요. 질문은 책의 내용에 기초합니다. 정답은 다음 페이지 하단에 있어요.

1
Where do ladybugs make their homes?
무당벌레는 어디에 집을 만드나요?

2
What do ladybugs eat?
무당벌레는 무엇을 먹나요?

3
How long do ladybugs live?
무당벌레는 얼마나 오래 사나요?

4
What happens to a ladybug's spots as they get older?
나이가 들면 무당벌레의 무늬는 어떻게 되나요?

5
What are aphids?
진딧물은 무엇인가요?

6
What flowers do most ladybugs like?
대부분 무당벌레는 어떤 꽃을 좋아하나요?

Explore other books in the Animals That Make a Difference series.

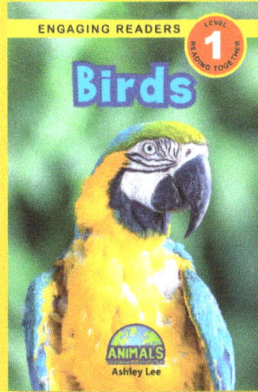

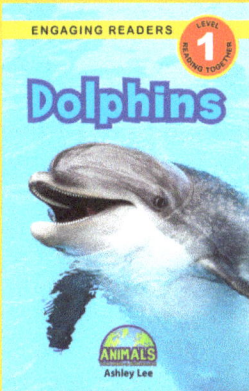

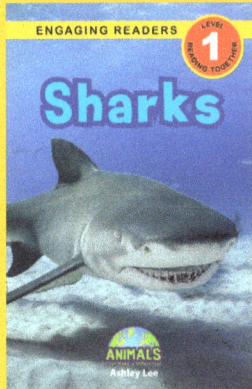

Bees
ENGAGING READERS — LEVEL 1 READING TOGETHER
ANIMALS That Make a Difference
Jared Siemens

Bats
ENGAGING READERS — LEVEL 1 READING TOGETHER
ANIMALS That Make a Difference
Ashley Lee

Birds
ENGAGING READERS — LEVEL 1 READING TOGETHER
ANIMALS That Make a Difference
Ashley Lee

Dolphins
ENGAGING READERS — LEVEL 1 READING TOGETHER
ANIMALS That Make a Difference
Ashley Lee

Horses
ENGAGING READERS — LEVEL 1 READING TOGETHER
ANIMALS That Make a Difference
Ashley Lee

Ladybugs
ENGAGING READERS — LEVEL 1 READING TOGETHER
ANIMALS That Make a Difference
Ashley Lee

Pigs
ENGAGING READERS — LEVEL 1 READING TOGETHER
ANIMALS That Make a Difference
Ashley Lee

Sharks
ENGAGING READERS — LEVEL 1 READING TOGETHER
ANIMALS That Make a Difference
Ashley Lee

Squirrels
ENGAGING READERS — LEVEL 1 READING TOGETHER
ANIMALS That Make a Difference
Ashley Lee

Visit www.engagebooks.com to explore more Engaging Readers.

정답: 1. 나무, 덤불 정원 2. 작은 벌레, 버섯과 나뭇잎 3. 2년에서 3년 4. 흐려져요 5. 사물을 먹고 곤충식사지는 작은 벌레 6. 마리골드, 코스모스, 카렌둘라

Answers: 1. In trees, bushes, or gardens 2. Smaller insects, mushrooms, and leaves 3. 2 to 3 years 4. They fade 5. Tiny bugs that eat and poison plants 6. Marigolds, cosmos, and calendula

31

www.ingramcontent.com/pod-product-compliance
Lightning Source LLC
Chambersburg PA
CBHW051238020426
42331CB00016B/3427